GW00836099

IMAGES OF ENGLAND

North Thanet Coast

This reprint is dedicated to the memory of the author, Alan Kay, who sadly passed away suddenly in July 2006, aged eighty-six.

IMAGES OF ENGLAND

North Thanet Coast

Alan Kay

NONSUCH

First published 1994
This new pocket edition 2006
Images unchanged from first edition

Nonsuch Publishing Limited
The Mill, Brimscombe Port,
Stroud, Gloucestershire, GL5 2QG
www.nonsuch-publishing.com

Nonsuch Publishing is an imprint of Tempus Publishing Group

British Library Cataloguing in Publication Data.
A catalogue record for this book is available from the British Library.

ISBN 1-84588-302-0

Typesetting and origination by Nonsuch Publishing Limited
Printed in Great Britain by Oaklands Book Services Limited

Contents

The ten-mile stretch of the North Thanet Coast consists of ten bays, each with its distinctive characteristics. They range from the crowded beaches of Margate (above) to the more secluded Botany Bay (below).

Introduction

There can be few ten-mile stretches of the English coastline with as varied a social or historical heritage as the North Thanet Coast, which has been mellowed by centuries of wind, rain, and storm tides. To the west is the Bronze Age site in Minnis Bay, the Saxon village of Birchington, and the 'private estate' of Westgate. Eastwards, we travel through Westbrook to the early seaside bathing resort of Margate, then to the contrasting socially upward development of Cliftonville. Finally, this stretch of coastline finishes at Botany Bay before turning south around North Foreland.

Before the early eighteenth century, there was just a small fishing hamlet at Margate on this stretch of coast with its ten bays. Much earlier, however, there was a Bronze Age site in Minnis Bay, Birchington, and small farming and fishing communities in rural Birchington and Gore End. Cliftonville to the east and Westgate to the west were not developed until the mid-nineteenth century. The population around the 1750s only totalled some 3,000 along this coastline where open fields met the sea.

By 1736, Margate developed into the country's first commercial sea bathing resort due to the popularity of drinking sea water and bathing in salt water as medicinal cures for most ailments. It then became the first resort to cater for social classes beneath the aristocracy, gentry, and clergy. For the first time, working-class artisans from the East End of London could visit the seaside using the cheap direct sail, and later steam, transport. In 1779, Cowper wrote,' ... there is lively company in Margate. Company, however, you would not want to be seen with'.

The vulgar and common reputation of visitors unashamedly enjoying drink and its associated pleasures led to the development of Cliftonville in 1867. Here, wealthier middle-class visitors were able to isolate themselves from the rough Cockney element in neighbouring Margate. A noticeable conflict of lifestyle and expectations became evident. Respectability was the keynote of Cliftonville – there, the boarding houses of Margate became private guest houses and hotels, dinner was served in the evening, and rough, amateur landladies were replaced by professional staff.

Westgate-on-Sea developed similarly; although adjoining Margate, it had nothing in common with it except the sea. In 1860 it was an area of open cornfields, but the wealthy Edmund Davies purchased 350 acres of land in the railway boom of 1878. He was an autocrat who approved all residents and their architectural designs. He planned 'a private town for wealthy Londoners' and erected gates to all the entry roads.

Westgate always prided itself on the discreet gentility and social exclusiveness of its residents. Davis did not want visitors and did nothing to attract them. Excursion trains were not allowed to stop at the station. Market forces later proved a harder task master, and by 1923 all the mortgaged land was put up for sale by the banks. The town still retained a selective individuality, however, much enjoyed by the large, retired element who enjoyed the ambience of a town first envisaged and planned by Edmund Davis in the 1880s.

Birchington, further west, has a history going back to Saxon times. Between the eleventh century and 1801 the population remained static at around 500, most of them employed by the local squire and farmer. The arrival of the railway in 1863 brought a great change with the development of the bracing cliff-top area attractive to a better class of resident in the new bungalow estates. It later enjoyed a reputation as a secluded sanatorium for invalids.

Post-war society has brought changes to the North Thanet Coast. There has been a partial rejection of the traditional bucket-and-spade, fortnight-by-the-sea holidays, and they have been replaced by increasing numbers of permanent residents enjoying their retirement years. With competition from continental holidays in the sun and the mobility which package tours and private car ownership bring, visitors have demanded a higher standard of amenities and seaside entertainment.

The long shoreline of ten miles is now haphazardly joined together by developments which have no separate local history behind them. The ten separate bays have enabled residents and visitors of different classes and different interests to spread laterally along the chalk cliffs. The coastal area here has never really adapted to the post-war cultural change in taste and in what people wanted from a holiday, although Margate has optimistic plans for the future to escape from its day tripper image.

Alan Kay
November 1994

One

The Ten Bays

The northern coast begins with Minnis Bay, Birchington, the site of an early Bronze Age settlement now eroded by the sea, but developed as a select seaside community at the turn of the century.

The chalk cliffs of North Thanet first make their appearance at Beresford Bay, Birchington — in Victorian times a haven for artists and literary people.

The next bay is Grenham Bay, the soft cliffs much eroded before coastal protection work took place.

Paddling at Epple Bay, Birchington-on-Sea.

Epple Bay, Birchington, at the turn of the century, showing the family holidays and the seaside gentility of Birchington.

A 1908 scene of West Bay, Westgate-on-Sea. A contemporary guide describes it as 'a healthy, genteel spot, but depressingly dull'.

The more popular Westgate bay is St Mildred's Bay. As the horizon shows, Westgate had not yet merged laterally into Margate in 1910. This development did not come until the 1920s.

The coastline of eroded inlets and bays leading from Westgate into Margate.

The curve of the coastline at Margate helped the town's development. Margate was a leading seaside resort particularly in Victorian and Edwardian times. By the 1980s both the Jetty and the Sun Deck had been removed.

Walpole Bay in 1913, the first bay in Cliftonville. Visitors in 1939 complained about paying 6d if they entered the sea without using the canvas tents or bathing cabins.

Palm Bay, to the east of Walpole Bay, became popular with the introduction of mixed bathing by the turn of the century. Previously, ladies and gentlemen had to be separated by lengthy spaces on the foreshore.

Foreness Bay, adjoining Palm Bay, Cliftonville. This attracted the quieter and more select visitor to an area which did nothing to attract the day trippers from Margate.

Proceeding eastwards, the chalk cliffs of the North Thanet coast increase in height. Erosion and coastal protection have always presented great problems to the area.

BOTANY BAY, KINGSGATE 644

The last bay on the North Thanet Coast is the secluded Botany Bay, possibly so named to remind local smugglers of punitive transportation to Australia should they be convicted.

Two

Contrasts in Development

The Sea Front Margate.

The ten-mile stretch of the North Thanet Coast shows great contrasts in the development of the various districts. As this 1906 card shows, Margate was unashamedly working-class, contrasting with the more select and class-conscious areas of Cliftonville, Westgate and Birchington.

1854 Margate
Queens Promenade

Cliftonville disassociated itself from its vulgar neighbour, Margate. Fashionable ladies were advised 'to pack at least 40 dresses for a holiday here'. This 1909 scene shows it was a place 'to see and be seen', enabling ladies to show off millinery and dresses to which the poorer class of visitor could not aspire.

The building of the Margate West railway station in 1863 enabled Margate to develop westwards into Westbrook. This shows the gracious line of guest houses in Royal Crescent, Westbrook, in 1907.

ROYAL CRESCENT, WESTBROOK, MARGATE.

Before 1914, Westgate-on-Sea was a haven of middle-class respectability compared with the seaside seediness of its neighbour to the east. Behaviour and dress code were important. Minstrels, hawkers and other distractions were not allowed by the Parochial Committee, who even had to approve the repertoire of numbers played by the ladies' orchestra.

The Bay & Promenade, Birchington-on-Sea

Birchington always endeavoured to remain aloof from its more popular neighbours. Visitors came here in search of health rather than amusement and pleasure. A favourite question on the promenade would be, 'What are you down here for?'

Margate Road, Birchington-on-Sea.

A mile inland, the rural village of Birchington huddled around the square, the parish church and four public houses.

Small villages were incorporated into the larger towns in 1913. One was Northdown, to the east of Cliftonville, linked by the tramway system from 1899 until 1936.

The lych gate of St Mary's church at Northdown in 1913. The Wheatsheaf Inn is at the far end of the road.

Salmestone Grange, whose chapel dates back to 1027, and Dent de Lion at Garlinge, with its fortified gateway and mansion dating back to the Middle Ages, are two historic buildings in the area.

Dent-de-Lion, Gateway Garling, Westgate-on-Sea

Three

Early Sea Bathing

Margate has the reputation of having been the first resort to introduce commercial sea bathing to the country in 1736. Medical opinion advocated both drinking and bathing in salt water as a cure for most common ills during the eighteenth century. The town's nearness to London, with regular direct sailing vessels, led to its increasing popularity, and an impetus was given by the invention of a local, Benjamin Beale, of a canvas modesty hood under which bathers had some privacy – bathing costumes not being common until mid-Victorian times.

Drinking and bathing in sea water were not sufficient diversions in themselves, so later came the establishment of bathing rooms, where visitors could socialise, read newspapers, listen to amateur musicians, and drink sherbet and eat jelly. The rooms occupied a line on the sea side of the Lower High Street, now converted into shops, as shown below.

For most of the nineteenth century visitors to this coast would come for the sea bathing. They would arrive by paddle steamers from wharves in the Tower Bridge area, and the Droit House, Margate, where the stone pier and jetty joined, would always be a scene of animation during the season. Several leading hotels were here, and local transport would take visitors to Westgate, Birchington, Cliftonville and across the island to Ramsgate.

Many forms of sea bathing could be seen along the North Thanet Coast. This 1908 card shows that day trippers would tend to paddle rather than hire bathing machines.

Longer-staying visitors would hire the ugly and baggy costumes from the bathing establishments. The serge or twill costumes would be washed out daily before being re-hired. In 1920, local byelaws decreed that everyone had to be fully covered between shoulder and knee.

It took some time before mixed bathing was accepted. This card from 1906 shows a policeman on horseback making sure the proprieties between the sexes were fully observed.

Some twenty years later, the bathing scene was much more relaxed. Groups from Cliftonville hotels would fraternise in water sports. One of the last lady 'dippers' to coax customers into the sea is shown on the right.

When the tide was out along the coast, bathers had to be carried out to undress in the bathing machines stationed offshore in a few feet of water.

The Bathing Parade, Margate.

Even when the tide was in, local boatmen would row bathers out. This 1920 card shows the crowded Pettman's Bathing Platform in front of the Cliftonville cliffs.

Epple Bay, Birchington-on-Sea.

For the first twenty years of this century, bathing at both Birchington and Westgate had to be undertaken from private canvas tents. Later visitors were allowed to indulge in 'mackintosh bathing', coming down to the beach from their hotels. Birchington ladies at Epple Bay would never paddle in the sea - only their nannies could do something so undignified.

Four

The Sands

The Sands again differentiate the atmosphere between the various bays along the coast. Margate Sands would always be bustling with activity and noise during the season. This 1902 card shows that male and female bathing machines were still separated.

In contrast, the sand scenes at Cliftonville, Westgate and Birchington would be far more decorous and less crowded. As this 1914 Cliftonville card shows, casual clothing for the beach had not yet made its appearance.

Events on Cliftonville Sands would often be organised in a civilised fashion. This photograph shows a ladies' keep fit class, with gentlemen also joining in, although the braces would perhaps be frowned upon as being more Margate than Cliftonville.

Cricket and sports competitions between the various guesthouses in Cliftonville would often be arranged on the sands.

There would be a variety of pastimes to be followed on the sands. Sand-castle building competitions would be organised, with valuable prizes. Others would listen to the pierrots or concert parties, paddling or taking donkey rides.

Church missions would come down to the sands every summer in an endeavour to catch the youngsters before they followed their parents into more secular and vulgar pursuits.

at Merry Margate

Even donkey rides show the differences between the towns. At 'merry Margate' the donkeys were often used by adults in races, with several local cases of prosecution by the RSPCA.

On the Sands, Westgate-on-Sea

At Westgate-on-Sea there were local byelaws restricting donkey rides to children under the age of fourteen.

This 1911 card shows that donkey rides in Cliftonville were often used as a fashion accessory. Even the donkey boy to the rights is dressed for the occasion. At Margate, ladies would sit astride but in Cliftonville it was *de rigueur* to sit side saddle.

At Westgate the parish council decreed that donkeys should be tethered with their rears facing the sea and facing the promenade.

5 30 51

These 1914 cards show that age did not seem to make much difference to London families paddling in the sea, or to parents helping their children sail model boats.

Margate was the first resort to introduce deckchairs to the sands, around the turn of the century. The first chairs were brought down by Edmund Atkins from the liners at Tilbury. Some fifteen made their appearance in 1898, but by 1906 over 2,000 were on Margate Sands.

This turn-of-the-century scene shows that before the deckchairs arrived local landladies would hire out their wooden kitchen chairs at hourly rates. Their children would bring the chairs down each day, and the legs would be inserted into boot polish tin lids to prevent them sinking into the sand.

The North Thanet Coast was always popular for family 'bucket and spade' holidays. The attraction was the clean golden sands, compared with the sharper shingle beaches around the coast.

A sand scene at Westgate in 1924 shows holiday clothing and push chairs typical of the period.

At Westgate the sands would not be so crowded, and the bathing machines with their ugly, hired costumes were not so popular. Bathing tents were introduced in Westgate, Birchington and Cliftonville. The nanny to the left would be a common sight on the sands at these places, but would rarely be seen on the sands at Margate.

This 1905 card shows 'grottoing' on the sands at Cliftonville. These would be sand designs carved out by a kitchen fork and embellished by seaweed and pebbles. Ostensibly, the local children collected coins for charities, but for many it was another form of pocket money.

Boating, Epple Bay, Birchington-on-Sea.

This 1905 card of Epple Bay, Birchington, shows a more genteel and formal atmosphere compared to the noisy, crowded beaches further east.

Local boatmen would run trips offshore. The most popular was the *Moss Rose*, which operated from 1890 until 1930.

Passengers enjoying a sea trip on the *Moss Rose* in 1928. The boat's inventory included mops and buckets in case of sea sickness. The holiday dress of the times often did not allow for this contingency.

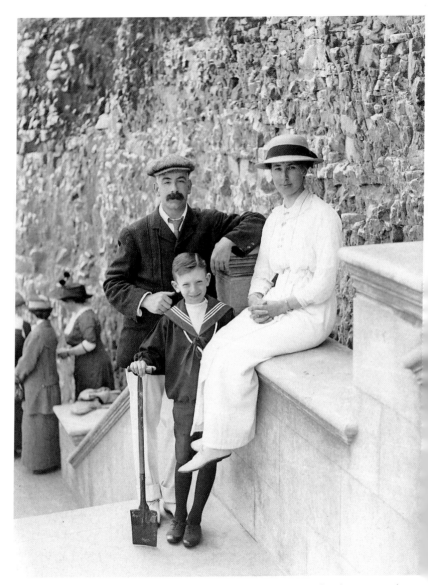

Dressed for a day on the sands at Westonville in 1920. Later, the name Westbrook was accepted for this district.

A 1921 scene at Westonville showing the bathing fashions of the day. The first personal, as opposed to hired, costumes make their appearance. The Bathing Pavilion shown here was opened in 1912.

At Margate the fashion was still the black or blue hired costumes from the bathing establishments.

J·971

Even as late as 1919 the bathing fashions on the sands at Minnis Bay, Birchington, were still appropriate to the decorum and gentility of this less favoured beach. An advertisement for Birchington stated one of its advantages to be that, 'it was much farther from Margate than Westgate'.

Five

Seaside Entertainments

Seaside entertainment has always centred on the more popular Margate. For many years both Westgate and Birchington would not allow minstrels, bands or concert parties—'We do not want to be as noisy as Margate'. Margate first featured black-faced minstrels in 1870. This shows a group entertaining outside the Britannia public house at the top of Fort Hill in 1886.

A local entertainer, Alfred Bourne, formed the 'Uncle Bones Margate Minstrels' in 1870. At first they did not have a regular base, but wandered along the sands where the greatest crowd could be found. They performed three times daily on the sands until the pierrots and concert parties took over before the First World War.

Later the minstrels moved along the sands to Cliftonville, but Westgate would only accept band concerts and Birchington frowned upon all noisy distractions breaking the peace and tranquillity of a holiday there.

By the early years of this century, pierrot groups had taken over from the minstrels. Harry Gold introduced his Margate Pierrots to the Marine Sands, providing a more sophisticated entertainment within a permanent stage setting.

Harry Gold (centre, back row) with his Margate Pierrots in 1905. The Pierrots had a standard costume of pointed caps, ruffled collars and black pom poms.

The pierrots were followed on the sands by the concert parties, with permanent staging, dressing rooms, and electric lighting. This lasted until the Second World War, after which the holiday public became more selective and demanding in their taste.

Margate had five bandstands by the turn of the century, occupied by touring military bands and resident concert parties. The Oval Bandstand, Cliftonville, shown here, became very popular, with several stars receiving their early stage training here.

The Bandstand, Westgate-on-Sea.

In 1903, Westgate built a Coronation Bandstand to celebrate the coronation of King Edward VII. Clearly from this photograph the public preferred free entertainment to paying for chairs.

Westbrook Bandstand, Margate

38141

Another popular bandstand was in Westbrook, a district developing westwards between 1880 and 1910.

The Westbrook bandstand was moved to Cliftonville in 1909, and the Westonville New Pavilion was opened in 1910 in its place. This enabled the seaside entertainment to be provided inside or out according to the vagaries of the English summer. The Pavilion was destroyed in the winter of 1953.

Another bandstand removed to make way for an indoor concert hall was on the Fort. This 1910 scene shows a London paddle steamer leaving from the Jetty.

The Fort was an area severely affected by the coastal erosion of the cliffs. The need to obtain hardcore for promenade protection works provided the impetus for the building of the Winter Gardens in 1911.

Some 70,000 cubic yards of chalk were dug out by pick and shovel and removed by horse and cart.

1975 Margate The Pavilion

In 1911 the Winter Gardens were built into the vast hole left by the excavations. To the left, scaffolding is still in position. The Concert Hall was designed with a stage opening both ways, the audience sitting on deckchairs in the open on the land side. In inclement weather the stage would face the covered interior on the sea side. The area around the Winter Gardens was then landscaped.

For many years Cecil Square was the centre of the town's entertainments. The original Assembly Rooms and Royal Hotel were built in 1769, and remained until the Great Fire of 1887.

After the fire the Grand Theatre was opened in 1898 on the Assembly Rooms corner of Cecil Square. Later, the name was changed to the Hippodrome, with the Regal Cinema adjoining. After a chequered career as a music hall, cinema and repertory theatre the building was demolished in 1967 to make way for the Municipal Offices and library.

A line of chorus girls from a touring Dudley Hippodrome company appearing in the Hippodrome in 1919, relaxing in their hired bathing costumes and caps.

Cinema-going was the main form of entertainment in pre-television days. The original Dreamland Cinema was converted from the Hall of Mirrors Ballroom in the Hall by the sea on the sea front.

Dreamland Cinema in 1920. The site was first planned as the sea front railway terminus in 1863, and the building became the Hall by the Sea when 'Lord' George Sanger took over in 1874. The building was demolished in 1936 when the present Dreamland Cinema opened.

Visits to the cinema were sometimes three and a half hours long, with two main films, interspersed with organ recitals, and one or two variety acts between the films. The Seven Dandy Lasses appeared there in 1927, and occasionally the Midgets would double with their performances in the Amusement Park.

These scenes show Dreamland Amusement Park when it was opened in 1919. It became a mecca for day trippers and works outings, sometimes providing 3,000 meals in its vast dining halls. Besides the usual sideshows and rides, there was a ballroom, skating rink, menagerie and cinema.

An added attraction staged in Dreamland would be a high diver diving into a small flaming tank. Tight-rope and trapeze acts in the Gardens would also be staged, with weekly firework displays.

Six

Early Transport

The early prosperity of the North Thanet Coast depended entirely on the cheap communication with London by the sea. Sailing hoys would be used until the first steam packets were introduced in 1815. The stone harbour pier could only be used at high tide, so in 1824 the Jarvis wooden jetty was built which enabled shipping to disembark and embark at all stages of the tide. The wooden jetty was replaced by an iron structure in 1855.

P.S. "ROYAL SOVEREIGN."

The last paddle steamers left Margate in 1956, but for 125 years paddle boats like the *Royal Sovereign* and *Royal Eagle* would leave Tower Bridge and Tilbury bringing their thousands down for the annual breaks by the sea.

SM602   P.S. ROYAL EAGLE APPROACHING TILBURY PIER ~ 19.8.1933

Pamlin Prints,
Croydon © 1970

Before private car ownership, the provision of public transport for the visitors was important. Horse brakes were very popular in Victorian times, as this photograph from crowded Marine Drive shows.

Rural trips by horse brakes to the picturesque villages of the Isle of Thanet were part of a seaside holiday. Tea gardens in Birchington, Minster and Pegwell were popular stops.

Wealthier visitors to Westbrook would hire private brakes. This 1910 photograph shows Tanting's team of greys outside the Nayland Rock Hotel.

Outside the luxury Cliftonville Hotel would be horse-drawn landaus, broughams, and a line of bath chairs for hire.

The Jetty, Margate

One attraction of a Thanet holiday some seventy-five years ago was a visit to France or Belgium on a day trip. The crowded jetty, 1910, illustrates the importance of the steamers to Margate. The steamers faced competition from the coming of the railway in 1846, and the direct line to London in 1863.

The railway changed the North Thanet Coast. Margate prospered most by having two stations on the sea front. Trains from the Margate Sands (above) went to London in 1846 via Ramsgate and Canterbury.

THE MARGATE STATION OF THE EAST KENT (LONDON, CHATHAM, AND DOVER) RAILWAY.

In 1863 a more direct line to Victoria was constructed, and the present Margate West Station was built.

Westgate-on-Sea was an example of a 'railway town'. The London to Thanet direct line led in 1863 to the building of a private town in open cornfields by the wealthy Edmund Davis. The town was for wealthy, middle class residents with servants, a complete contrast to Margate. No day tripper would be allowed in Westgate.

Westgate-on-Sea station has hardly changed in a hundred years. Originally, the trains to Westgate were exclusive trains for exclusive residents. The station has not changed through the years, although the class of resident is now more mixed.

Plans for a railway station in Cliftonville were abandoned in 1913, although a small station was opened to serve the development of East Margate. This station was closed down in 1953.

Birchington also developed through the railway line after 1863. Previously a rural village two miles inland, the railway allowed the development of the cliff top area between the station and the sea.

Trams were introduced to the island in 1899. This shows the terminus at the end of George V Avenue, Garlinge, where a ten-minute service commenced at 5.30am and rumbled through Broadstairs to Ramsgate.

Margate.   The Marine Parade.

This 1906 card shows a tram and horse brakes on The Parade. At that time this was the busiest part of Margate with the Jetty and some of the leading hotels.

Between the wars, open-topped charabancs with solid tyres and wooden seats were popular with visitors for their days out to neighbouring towns. They were also used for club outings, as this 1921 photograph of Cecil Square shows.

In this card of 1925 many different forms of transport may be seen around the Jubilee Clock Tower, built for Queen Victoria's Jubilee in 1889. The transport ranges from horse-drawn carts and brakes, to private cars, taxis, charabancs, and electric trams.

Seven

Contrasts in Architecture

Like so many heritage towns, the architecture illustrates the social changes which have taken place over the years. Marine Terrace originally comprised graceful Victorian apartment houses which would be leased for the season. The need to accommodate large, wealthy families with their servants explains their height and appearance.

By the turn of the century the ground floors were converted into shop and cafes. Some fifty years later these were superseded by the 'Golden Mile' of electronic games arcades, neon lights, and synthetic music.

In contrast with raucous working-class atmosphere of Margate was the growth of graceful terraces and quality hotels in Cliftonville to the east in the 1880s. This district catered for middle-class society, 'who would never want to be seen in Margate'.

Westgate-on-Sea to the west shows a similar contrast, deliberately cutting itself off from the noisy pleasure-seeking visitors to Margate. Originally planned by Davis as a private estate, it developed in Victorian times into a seaside haven of large, detached houses individually designed for wealthy owners. During the twentieth century most of these have been converted into private schools, convalescent homes, and private hotels.

One house later converted into a hotel was Rowena Court, on the corner of Sea Road with Westbrook Avenue. The corner site was the home of local benefactors Sir Erasmus Wilson and Sir William Ingram. In 1966 the hotel was demolished and replaced by a modern housing development.

Two miles to the west of Westgate is Birchington, which was originally a rural community with a village green, fountain, and public houses around the parish church. This 1912 scene may easily be reconciled with the present day.

The railway brought about the extension of Birchington between the original inland village and the sea. The architect J.P. Seddon designed the country's first bungalow estate on the cliff top. The hotel near the station was built in 1881, and it remained very much unchanged until it was demolished in 1987 to make way for the Bierce Court Retirement Homes.

The architect Seddon had many friendships with London's literary and artistic circles. Sir George Frampton's bungalow, shown here in 1912, had many attractive frescoes. Frampton was the Victorian sculptor who designed the Peter Pan statue in London.

Solomon J. Solomon, R.A. was another Victorian artist who owned a bungalow in Birchington. Most of the bungalows on the cliff top had private steps leading down to the beach at Grenham Bay.

Rossetti Bungalow, Birchington-on-Sea

Dante Gabriel Rossetti, the Victorian painter, came to Birchington for his health, and died here in 1882. His grave is in Birchington churchyard. The Rossetti Bungalow was demolished in 1966.

The Clyffe, Sea View Road, Birchington-on-Sea.

A 1928 photograph of the Clyffe Bungalow on the Bungalow Estate.

Later development moved westwards along the coast. This 1900 scene of Minnis Bay shows the newly-built Bay Hotel, and the 'colonial terrace' to the right built for retired British Empire builders.

Before the railway came in 1863, Birchington village was completely separated from the other settlements on the North Thanet Coast. As this 1912 scene shows, the main street could always be crossed in complete safety.

The gracious uniformity of late eighteenth-century crescents is still evident in Union Crescent, Margate. Originally one of the best addresses in the town, most of the houses were leased by members of the aristocracy. Nowadays, it has unfortunately deteriorated into a line of cheaper boarding houses and multi-occupancy flatlets.

Eight

Local Victorian Entrepeneurs

Before multiple chain stores invaded our high streets, it was left to local businessmen to provide a varied range of goods. Margate's F.J. Bobby started with one shop in the High Street in 1887. In 1898, he had expanded into the area's first department store. By 1915 he had established branches in seven other seaside resorts. Debenhams took over the company in 1968, and the premises were closed down in 1972.

The Pettmans were another local family showing business initiative. In 1860, Pettman built a bathing platform at Cliftonville, later developed by Charlotte, his daughter. By the 1920s the firm had expanded their interests into an ice cream factory, removals, coal merchants, fruit stalls, and beach photography.

A bathing party leaving Pettman's bathing platform in 1925.

The Pettman family had the bathing monopoly in Cliftonville, while the Perkins family had similar concessions in Margate. They introduced deck chairs to the beach, and hired the bathing machines off Marine Terrace.

Marine Terrace in 1904 with the lines of Perkins bathing machines, the trams, the horse brakes, and to the right the entrances to the two sea front railway stations, Margate Sands and Margate West.

Another Pettman enterprise was the Sunbeam Photo Company, the first large photographic studio in England. Between the wars their wandering photographers took thousands of photographs of happy holidaymakers on the beaches between Cliftonville and Westgate. The display screens would be scanned avidly the following morning and orders placed.

Like many small hotels and shops, most restaurants and tea rooms between the wars were owned by local families. This 1909 photograph shows the 'Koh-I-Noor', the end of a popular walk along the cliffs at Cliftonville. Later this was known as the Bungalow Restaurant, destroyed by fire in 1992.

DANE PARK MARGATE

Many local businessmen prospered from the seaside industry. They later proved to be generous benefactors to the town. Among these was John Woodward, who donated the farmland to make Dane Park in 1896.

Lewis Avenue, Cliftonville

75015.JV

Many local hoteliers prospered by starting in one or two buildings, then using their profits to expand into adjoining properties. This shows the St Georges Hotel in 1914, which was first established by the Cleveland family in one house in 1899. By 1924 the family had purchased the fourteen adjoining properties to make one integrated hotel. This was purchased by Butlins in 1955.

This 1912 photograph shows that the sea front along this coast offered much scope for local businessmen to prosper. The sands would be crowded with bathing machine touts, donkey men, itinerant hawkers of ice cream and fruit, sweet and magazine kiosks, organ grinders, and performing animals. Local families rather than national companies would be in charge of the restaurants, souvenir shops, and public houses which faced this busy scene.

Nine

Demolition and Renovation

An important function of old photographs is to show areas which have changed out of all recognition due to demolition for housing development or road widening schemes. Cranbourne Alley, shown here, between Hawley Square and St John's Church, was demolished in the road widening scheme of 1952.

Cecil Square, Margate, is another area which has changed out of recognition. The post office building remains, but the Hippodrome Theatre has been replaced by modern offices, and the Square is now a hub of traffic congestion. This photograph from 1925 illustrates the change.

Every building shown in this 1910 photograph has now gone, all were swept away in the 1938 Fort Hill improvement scheme which provided the present attractive dual carriageway sweeping down to The Parade.

Like so many coastal areas, many buildings were bombed during the Second World War and now only remain as nostalgic memories to older residents. Among these was Margate College, a minor public school on a tree-lined site in Hawley Street, originally built in 1886 and bombed in 1942. It has now been replaced by the concrete of a supermarket car park and its attendant stores.

Holy Trinity Church, built in 1826, was another wartime casualty. Destroyed in a hit-and-run air raid in July 1943, the site is now a car park.

The impressive interior of Holy Trinity church.

Cliftonville has suffered greatly from the decline in quality hotels. The 250-room Cliftonville Hotel, built in 1868, catered for wealthy visitors who would come down with servants and carriages. The hotel was demolished in 1961, and the site is now a bowling alley.

Another hotel demolished in 1985 was the Queens Highcliffe Hotel. The hotel has now been replaced by the Queens Court housing development.

THE BERESFORD HOTEL, BIRCHINGTON-ON-SEA, KENT.

Birchington also suffered through the closing of first-class hotels. The luxury Beresford Hotel on the cliff top was demolished in 1967 and a new estate was laid out.

Published by I. Venis, The Library, Westgate-on-Sea.

This trend was also evident on the front at Westgate. Many Victorian hotels were converted into convalescent homes and private schools. However, Ledge Point has now reverted to a hotel from a nursing home.

Margate also lost important hotels through closure or demolition. The White Hart Hotel on The Parade was a leading hotel in Victorian times. Disraeli, Gladstone, and Lord Beaconsfield all stayed here. The building was demolished in 1960, and the site is now occupied by White Hart Mansions.

Road widening schemes have also changed the landscape. The main entrance to North Thanet from London came through Birchington past the village pond in Canterbury Road. The road was widened in 1933 and the pond was filled in.

At Westgate, the main road was quite narrow, passing through open fields, until the increase in private car ownership and day tripper coaches between the wars caused a dual carriageway to be constructed for most of the way.

Workmen on the road widening scheme in Birchington in March 1933. The lack of mechanical machinery is noticeable, the work being largely manual and waste carried away by horse and cart. The parish church of All Saints, dating from early Norman times, is in the background.

Windmills were once a striking sight on the skyline. The Drapers Mills shown here in 1900 originally had three mills. Now just one remains, refurbished by a group of enthusiastic volunteers.

The old Tudor Cottage in King Street was renovated in 1951 after war damage. The 1920 photograph shows the original cottages occupied by local seafarers since the seventeenth century. The beams and plasterwork remain in good condition.

WEST GATE-ON-SEA — Autour du Pensionnat des Dames Ursulines

Originally individual communities with individual histories separated by open fields, the ten-mile stretch of coastline consisting of Cliftonville, Margate, Westgate, and Birchington is now joined laterally into a long strip of residential development. This 1912 photograph shows sheep grazing near the Ursuline Convent on open land between Westgate and Birchington.

Ten

Miscellany

Through the centuries the North Thanet Coast has been subjected to many severe winter storms. The piers have been reconstructed several times. In 1977 Margate Jetty was completely destroyed and all that now remains are a few rusting girders jutting above the waves. The wooden planking of the Jetty was washed up on Marine Terrace after the great storm.

In 1897, another storm destroyed the Marine Palace shown here below Fort Hill to the east of the harbour. The piano belonging to the dance hall was washed ashore over a mile away.

The constant pounding of the waves on the soft chalk cliffs meant that coastal protection works were essential if hotels and other buildings were not to collapse into the sea.

WESTGATE - LOOKING WEST. WESTGATE - ON - SEA.

All along this northern coastline it was necessary to build sea walls and promenades. This 1907 photograph shows the new promenade at St Mildred's Bay, Westgate-on-Sea.

NEW PROMENADE, MINNIS BAY, BIRCHINGTON.

K.6836

Now practically the whole ten-mile stretch of coastline from Minnis Bay, Birchington, to Foreness Bay, Cliftonville, has some form of coastal protection.

An added attraction was the cliff top walks above the promenades, as these 1910 photographs of Westgate show. They also illustrate the Edwardian dress favoured by visitors to this resort.

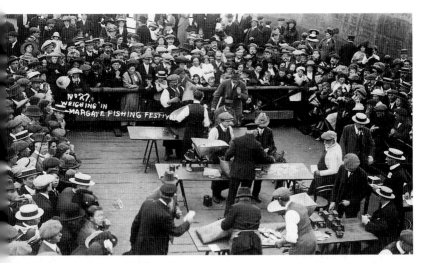

Fishing has always been important along this coastline, both for full-time fishermen and the amateurs enjoying their hobby. This shows 'weighing in' at the 1929 Margate Fishing Competition on the Jetty.

Margate has had a harbour since the fourteenth century, and before rail and road transport all visitors and heavy goods entered here. This shows the busy scene in 1913, but sadly in recent times silting has occurred and now only a few small local boats are moored here.

After the opening of the gas works in 1824, a regular harbour sight would be colliers from the Tyne bringing in gascoal. This ceased with the introduction of North Sea gas in 1958.

The Jetty was an important part of the Margate seascape until its destruction in the storms of 1977. This 1910 scene shows the *Royal Eagle* paddle steamer, and part of the Naval fleet offshore. The crowded holiday resort would be used for recruiting and publicity purposes each summer when battleships and cruisers would anchor offshore for local visits.

This coast has always enjoyed a reputation for bracing health-providing air. This was given an impetus in 1791 when the Royal Sea Bathing Hospital was built in Westbrook, the first specialised hospital in the country.

Dating from 1910, in this photograph the Royal Sea Bathing Hospital can be seen in the background. London children would be sent down for the sea-water and sea-air cure to help relieve lung and bone consumption.

Many of the large private mansions and private hotels along the coast were converted into convalescent homes. A good example is the Royal Oak Convalescent Home in Westgate, at one time a terrace of private guest houses.

In Northdown Road, Cliftonville, was the West Ham Convalescent Home, a healthy seaside haven for invalid children from the East End of London. At one time there were over forty convalescent homes in Thanet.

Taking advantage of Thanet's health-giving qualities was the establishment of private preparatory schools and ladies' colleges. By 1922 it was estimated that between 3,000 and 5,000 children were sent annually to these local boarding schools. Hynton House School was on the sea front at Cliftonville.

Westgate-on-Sea had thirty private schools before the First World War. This photograph shows the spartan classroom typical of schools of this period.

To reassure parents who feared fire dangers some schools would produce photographs showing pupils at fire drill, as this 1906 advertisement shows. The iron brackets used to support the ladders are still visible on this house in Northdown Road, Cliftonville.

This 1903 photographs shows that private boarding schools would often occupy premises originally built as private hotels in late Victorian times, when holiday accommodation was over-estimated.

Small classes were the norm. Middle-class parents would send their children to Westgate schools for the healthy air and gentility of the district.

Some of the staff of the St Margaret Ladies School on Sea Road, Westgate-on-Sea, in October 1918.

Northdown House is a typical example of a mansion built for wealthy farmers and landowners. This turn-of-the-century photograph shows members of the Friend family. In 1937 they sold the house and estate to Margate Corporation to make a public park.

Another mansion in the area is Quex Mansion, Birchington. This was the home of the Powell-Cottons. During the late nineteenth century the owner was a big game hunter and collector. A museum has been established to exhibit panoramas of wild animals and other artefacts from his journeys into Africa and Asia.

During the First World War mansions such as Quex would be used by the Red Cross for the rehabilitation of wounded soldiers.

"The Thicket", Birchington-on-Sea.

In Birchington, large private houses would be used for the same purpose. 'The Thickett' was opened by Dr Cross as a convalescent home for wounded officers of the Household Cavalry, his old regiment. Later, this road was named Cross Road.

Carmelcourt, Birchington, Kent.

Many buildings have disappeared over the years to make way for modern developments. A block of flats now occupies the site of Carmel Court in Birchington. This 1911 photograph shows Carmel Court, a copy of a building on Mount Carmel, near Haifa, Israel.

Westonville Pavilion, Margate

An entertainment centre no longer visible is the Westbrook Pavilion, the venue for many pre-war stars. It was severely damaged in a storm in 1949, necessitating its demolition. With the change in visitors' entertainment tastes, it was never replaced.

Many improvements were made along this coast between the wars, and impressive opening ceremonies would be staged. This shows the Prince of Wales (later the Duke of Windsor) opening the Prince's Walk Promenade in Cliftonville in 1926.

Part of North Thanet's sporting history was made when Arsenal adopted Margate Football Club as their 'nursery' club. Five in this group later played in the Arsenal first team; two played for Wales, and one for England.

Many gaps were cut through the chalk. Most were cut by early farmers to collect seaweed to fertilise their fields before chemical fertilisers. Now they are used by visitors to reach the foreshore.

Coast Guard Station, Birchington Bay. 98.

Smuggling was rife along the North Thanet Coast during the eighteenth and early nineteenth centuries, and these gaps in the coast provided an easy entry inland. Customs posts were built and later converted into coastguard stations, as this 1910 photograph of Birchington Bay shows.

This 1904 photograph of the village pond at Birchington shows the first private car to be owned in Thanet. There is a local dispute as to whether this was owned by a Dr White or the Redman family. The car is a solid tyred Benz.

When the communities were separated by open fields, public houses and tea gardens were pleasant stops for trips into the country. The Hussar Hotel and Tea Gardens at Garlinge is shown in this 1914 photograph.

The Walmer Castle on Streete Court Hill is another public house which was built in Victorian times as a stop on the road leading into Westgate.

The Tower House Convent was built in 1898 as a home for alcoholics. Since then, it has been Les Oiseaux Convent for French nuns, the Tower House Convent, an exclusive girls' school, and, since 1972, the Abbey School.

This photograph dating from 1919 shows the building of sea defences at Minnis Bay, Birchington.

Acknowledgements

For factual assistance, thanks to Penny Ward, Heritage Officer, Margate Public Library, and John Williams, Margate Old Town Museum.

8626 GRENHAM BAY, BIRCHINGTON